Normalizing Monetary Policy: Prospects and Perspectives

March 27, 2015

Page Intentionally Left Blank

Page Intentionally Left Blank

Page Intentionally Left Blank

I would like to thank President Williams for his kind introduction and the Federal Reserve Bank of San Francisco for inviting me to what promises to be a very stimulating and important conference.

As you know, last week the Federal Open Market Committee (FOMC) changed its forward guidance pertaining to the federal funds rate. With continued improvement in economic conditions, an increase in the target range for that rate may well be warranted later this year. Of course, the timing of the first increase in the federal funds rate and its subsequent path will be determined by the Committee in light of incoming data on labor market conditions, inflation, and other aspects of the current expansion.

In my remarks today I will discuss some factors that will likely guide our decisions as we adjust the stance of monetary policy over time. I will also discuss why most of my colleagues and I believe the return of the federal funds rate to a more normal level is likely to be gradual. In doing so, I will address three questions. First, why does the Committee judge that an increase in the federal funds rate target is likely to become appropriate later this year? Second, how are economic and financial considerations likely to shape the course of monetary policy over the next several years? And, finally, are there special risks and other considerations that policymakers should take into account in the current environment?

Current Economic Conditions and the Outlook

Before turning to these questions, however, let me first review where the economy is now and where it's likely headed--a necessary backdrop for understanding why, after more than six years of maintaining a near-zero federal funds rate and accumulating a large portfolio of longer-term securities, the Committee is now giving serious consideration to beginning to reduce later this year some of the extraordinary monetary policy accommodation currently in place.

Although the recovery of the labor market from the deep recession following the financial crisis was frustratingly slow for quite a long time, progress has been more rapid of late. The unemployment rate has fallen markedly over the past few years and now stands at 5.5 percent, down from 10 percent at its peak. Payroll gains have averaged 275,000 per month over the past year, well above the pace needed to sustain further declines in the unemployment rate. Of course, we still have some way to go to reach our maximum employment goal. The unemployment rate has not yet declined to the 5.0 to 5.2 percent range that most FOMC participants now consider to be normal in the longer run. Involuntary part-time employment remains high by historical standards. Labor force participation is still somewhat lower than I would expect after accounting for demographic trends.[1] And wage growth continues to be quite subdued. But I think we can all agree that the recovery in the labor market has been substantial.

I am cautiously optimistic that, in the context of moderate growth in aggregate output and spending, labor market conditions are likely to improve further in coming months. In particular, and despite the somewhat disappointing tone of the recent retail

---

[1] For a discussion of the influence of demographics and other factors on the labor force participation rate in recent years, see Stephanie Aaronson, Tomaz Cajner, Bruce Fallick, Felix Galbis-Reig, Christopher Smith, and William Wascher (2014), "Labor Force Participation: Recent Developments and Future Prospects," Brookings Papers on Economic Activity (Washington: Brookings Institution, Fall), www.brookings.edu/about/projects/bpea/papers/2014/labor-force-participation-recent-developments-and-future-prospects. In addition, for evidence that the labor force participation rate is currently unusually low from a cyclical perspective, see Robert E. Hall (2014), "Quantifying the Lasting Harm to the U.S. Economy from the Financial Crisis," in Jonathan Parker and Michael Woodford, eds., NBER Macroeconomics Annual 2014, vol. 29 (Chicago: University of Chicago Press); and Council of Economic Advisers (2014), "The Labor Force Participation Rate since 2007: Causes and Policy Implications" (Washington: CEA, July), www.whitehouse.gov/sites/default/files/docs/labor_force_participation_report.pdf.

sales data, I think consumer spending is likely to expand at a good clip this year given such robust fundamentals as strong employment gains, boosts to real incomes from lower energy prices, continued increases in household wealth, and a relatively high level of consumer confidence. Of course, not all sectors of the economy are doing as well: dollar appreciation appears to be restraining net exports, low oil prices are prompting a cutback in drilling activity, and the recovery in residential construction remains subdued. But overall, I anticipate that real gross domestic product is likely to expand somewhat faster than its potential in coming quarters, thereby promoting further gains in employment and declines in the unemployment rate.

In assessing the actual strength of the labor market and the broader economy, we must bear in mind that these very welcome improvements have been achieved in the context of extraordinary monetary accommodation. While the overall level of real activity now appears to be much closer to its potential than it was a year or two ago, the economy in an "underlying" sense remains quite weak by historical standards, for the simple reason that the increases in hiring and output that have been achieved thus far have required exceptionally low levels of short- and longer-term interest rates, reflecting a highly accommodative stance of monetary policy. Interest rates have been, and remain, very low, and if underlying conditions had truly returned to normal, the economy should be booming. As I will discuss shortly, this assessment concerning the underlying strength of real activity has important policy implications.

While there has been considerable progress on the maximum employment leg of our dual mandate, progress on the price stability leg has been notably absent. Inflation as measured by the price index for personal consumption expenditures has been running below the FOMC's longer-run goal of 2 percent for a number of years, and on a

12-month basis is currently 1/4 percent. Some of the weakness in inflation likely reflects

continuing slack in labor and product markets. However, much of this weakness stems

from the sharp decline in the price of oil and other one-time factors that, in the FOMC's

judgment, are likely to have only a transitory negative effect on inflation, provided that

inflation expectations remain well anchored.

In this regard, I take comfort from the continued stability of survey measures of

longer-run inflation expectations. And although market-based measures of inflation

compensation have declined appreciably since last summer and bear close watching, I

suspect that these declines are primarily driven by changes in risk premiums and market

factors that I expect to prove transitory. On balance, I therefore think it is appropriate for

monetary policy to remain accommodative for some time, fostering an environment of

tightening labor and product markets that, together with stable inflation expectations, will

help move inflation up to 2 percent over the medium term.

Why Might an Increase in the Federal Funds Rate Be Warranted Later This Year?

The Committee's decision about when to begin reducing accommodation will

depend importantly on how economic conditions actually evolve over time. Like most of

my FOMC colleagues, I believe that the appropriate time has not yet arrived, but I expect

that conditions may warrant an increase in the federal funds rate target sometime this

year. So let me spell out the reasoning that underpins this view.

I would first note that the current stance of monetary policy is clearly providing

considerable economic stimulus. The near-zero setting for the federal funds rate has

facilitated a sizable reduction in labor market slack over the past two years and appears to be consistent with further substantial gains. A modest increase in the federal funds rate would be highly unlikely to halt this progress, although such an increase might slow its pace somewhat.

Second, we need to keep in mind the well-established fact that the full effects of monetary policy are felt only after long lags. This means that policymakers cannot wait until they have achieved their objectives to begin adjusting policy. I would not consider it prudent to postpone the onset of normalization until we have reached, or are on the verge of reaching, our inflation objective. Doing so would create too great a risk of significantly overshooting *both* our objectives of maximum sustainable employment and 2 percent inflation, potentially undermining economic growth and employment if the FOMC is subsequently forced to tighten policy markedly or abruptly. In addition, holding rates too low for too long could encourage inappropriate risk-taking by investors, potentially undermining the stability of financial markets. That said, we must be reasonably confident at the time of the first rate increase that inflation will move up over time to our 2 percent objective, and that such an action will not impede continued solid growth in employment and output.

An important factor working to increase my confidence in the inflation outlook will be continued improvement in the labor market. A substantial body of theory, informed by considerable historical evidence, suggests that inflation will eventually begin to rise as resource utilization continues to tighten.[2] It is largely for this reason that a

---

[2] For recent evidence on the relationship between labor market slack and wages, see Anil Kumar and Pia Orrenius (2014), "A Closer Look at the Phillips Curve Using State Level Data," Working Papers 1409 (Dallas: Federal Reserve Bank of Dallas), www.dallasfed.org/assets/documents/research/papers/2014/wp1409.pdf; and Daniel Aaronson and Andrew Jordan (2014), "Understanding the Relationship between Real Wage Growth and Labor Market Conditions," Chicago Fed Letter No. 327 (Chicago: Federal Reserve Bank of Chicago, October), www.chicagofed.org/publications/chicago-fed-letter/2014/october-327. The price Phillips curve is

significant pickup in incoming readings on core inflation will *not* be a precondition for me to judge that an initial increase in the federal funds rate would be warranted. With respect to wages, I anticipate that real wage gains for American workers are likely to pick up to a rate more in line with trend labor productivity growth as employment settles in at its maximum sustainable level. We could see nominal wage growth eventually running notably higher than the current roughly 2 percent pace. But the outlook for wages is highly uncertain even if price inflation does move back to 2 percent and labor market conditions continue to improve as projected. For example, we cannot be sure about the future pace of productivity growth; nor can we be sure about other factors, such as global competition, the nature of technological change, and trends in unionization, that may also influence the pace of real wage growth over time. These factors, which are outside of the Federal Reserve's control, likely explain why real wages have failed to keep pace with productivity growth for at least the past 15 years. For such reasons, we can never be sure what growth rate of nominal wages is consistent with stable consumer price inflation, and this uncertainty limits the usefulness of wage trends as an indicator of the Fed's progress in achieving its inflation objective.

I have argued that a pickup in neither wage nor price inflation is indispensable for me to achieve reasonable confidence that inflation will move back to 2 percent over time. That said, I would be uncomfortable raising the federal funds rate if readings on wage

---

discussed extensively in the literature; for instance, see Robert J. Gordon (2013), "The Phillips Curve Is Alive and Well: Inflation and the NAIRU during the Slow Recovery," NBER Working Paper Series 19390 (Cambridge, Mass.: National Bureau of Economic Research, August). In addition, the apparent lack of disinflationary pressure seen during the recent recession is not necessarily a puzzle for the New Keynesian Phillips curve, as shown in Marco Del Negro, Marc P. Giannoni, and Frank Schorfheide (2015), "Inflation in the Great Recession and New Keynesian Models," *American Economic Journal: Macroeconomics*, vol. 7 (January), pp. 168-96.

growth, core consumer prices, and other indicators of underlying inflation pressures were to weaken, if market-based measures of inflation compensation were to fall appreciably further, or if survey-based measures were to begin to decline noticeably.

Under normal circumstances, simple monetary policy rules, such as the one proposed by John Taylor, could help us decide when to raise the federal funds rate.[3] Even with core inflation running below the Committee's 2 percent objective, Taylor's rule now calls for the federal funds rate to be well above zero if the unemployment rate is currently judged to be close to its normal longer-run level and the "normal" level of the real federal funds rate is currently close to its historical average. But the prescription offered by the Taylor rule changes significantly if one instead assumes, as I do, that appreciable slack still remains in the labor market, and that the economy's equilibrium real federal funds rate--that is, the real rate consistent with the economy achieving maximum employment and price stability over the medium term--is currently quite low by historical standards.[4] Under assumptions that I consider more realistic under present circumstances, the same rules call for the federal funds rate to be close to zero.[5]

---

[3] For the original exposition of the Taylor rule, see John B. Taylor (1993), "Discretion Versus Policy Rules in Practice," *Carnegie-Rochester Conference Series on Public Policy,* vol. 39, pp. 195-214. For a discussion of policy rules in general, see John B. Taylor and John C. Williams (2010), "Simple and Robust Rules for Monetary Policy," in Benjamin M. Friedman and Michael Woodford, eds., *Handbook of Monetary Economics,* vol. 3B (San Diego: Elsevier), pp. 829-59.

[4] The equilibrium real rate is typically viewed as the level of the short-term interest rate, less inflation, estimated to be consistent with maximum employment and stable inflation in the long run, assuming no future disturbances to the economy. Accordingly, the equilibrium real rate is usually thought of as independent of the cyclical disturbances that routinely buffet the economy, on the assumption that the influences of such disturbances on real activity and inflation fade away after a few years. In the aftermath of the financial crisis, however, the U.S. economy has been subject to various adjustment processes that are unusually drawn out by historical standards, such as the ongoing repair of household balance sheets and other persistent headwinds. These atypical processes imply that, in determining the appropriate stance of monetary policy over time, policymakers in the current environment need to take account of slow-moving influences on both aggregate demand and supply that were not important factors during previous tightening episodes. For this reason, it is useful to think of the equilibrium real rate in present circumstances as not only time-varying but also having a predictable element that evolves over the medium term.

[5] For example, the Taylor rule is $R_t = RR^* + \pi_t + 0.5(\pi_t - 2) + 0.5Y_t$, where R denotes the federal funds rate, RR^* is the estimated value of the equilibrium real rate, π is the current inflation rate (usually measured

Moreover, I would assert that simple rules are, well, too simple, and ignore important complexities of the current situation, about which I will have more to say shortly.

The FOMC will, of course, carefully deliberate about when to begin the process of removing policy accommodation. But the significance of this decision should not be overemphasized, because what matters for financial conditions and the broader economy is the entire expected path of short-term interest rates and not the precise timing of the first rate increase. The spending and investment decisions the FOMC seeks to influence depend primarily on expectations of policy well into the future, as embedded in longer-term interest rates and other asset prices. More important than the timing of the Committee's initial policy move will be the strategy the Committee deploys in adjusting the federal funds rate over time, in response to economic developments, to achieve its dual mandate. Market participants' perceptions of that reaction function and the implications for the likely longer-run trajectory of short-term interest rates will influence the borrowing costs faced by households and businesses, including the rates on corporate bonds, auto loans, and home mortgages.

How Are Economic and Financial Considerations Likely to Shape the Course of Monetary Policy over the Next Several Years?

Let me therefore turn to the second question I posed earlier: How are economic and financial considerations likely to shape the course of monetary policy over the next

---

using a core consumer price index), and Y is the output gap. The latter can be approximated using Okun's law, $Y_t = -2(U_t - U^*)$, where U is the unemployment rate and U^* is the natural rate of unemployment. If RR^* is assumed to equal 2 percent (roughly the average historical value of the real federal funds rate) and U^* is assumed to equal 5-1/2 percent, then the Taylor rule would call for the nominal funds rate to be set a bit below 3 percent currently, given that core PCE inflation is now running close to 1-1/4 percent and the unemployment rate is 5.5 percent. But if RR* is instead assumed to equal 0 percent currently (as some statistical models suggest) and U* is assumed to equal 5 percent (an estimate in line with many FOMC participants' SEP projections), then the rule's current prescription is less than 1/2 percent.

few years? Let me first be clear that the FOMC does not intend to embark on any predetermined course of tightening following an initial decision to raise the funds rate target range--one that, for example, would involve similarly sized rate increases at every meeting or on some other schedule. Rather, the actual path of policy will evolve as economic conditions evolve, and policy tightening could speed up, slow down, pause, or even reverse course depending on actual and expected developments in real activity and inflation. Reflecting such data dependence, as well as some historically unusual policy considerations that I will discuss shortly, the average pace of tightening observed during previous recoveries could well provide a highly misleading guide to the actual course of monetary policy over the next few years. Our goal in adjusting the federal funds rate over time will be to achieve and sustain economic conditions close to maximum employment with inflation averaging around 2 percent, responding, as best we can, to the inevitable twists and turns of the economy.

Keeping in mind the all-important proviso that policy is never predetermined but is always data dependent, what can we say about the appropriate path of policy, assuming the most likely outcomes for real activity, inflation, and related factors? The answer is that it depends, of course, on one's outlook for the economy. Today I will focus on the modal outlook presented by FOMC participants' submissions to the March Summary of Economic Projections (SEP), which assumes that no further unanticipated disturbances buffet the economy. As I noted at my press conference after last week's FOMC meeting, participants generally project that the unemployment rate will continue to fall through late 2017 to levels at or somewhat below estimates of its longer-run sustainable level, accompanied by growth in real gross domestic product that runs somewhat above its estimated longer-run trend with inflation moving up to around 2 percent. This solid economic performance is projected to be consistent with a gradual normalization of monetary policy: The median funds rate projection in the March SEP increases a percentage point per year on average through the end of 2017.

The projected combination of a gradual rise in the nominal federal funds rate coupled with further progress on both legs of the dual mandate is consistent with an implicit assessment by the Committee that the equilibrium real federal funds rate--one measure of the economy's underlying strength--is rising only slowly over time. In the wake of the financial crisis, the equilibrium real rate apparently fell well below zero because of numerous persistent headwinds. These headwinds include tighter underwriting standards and restricted access to some forms of credit; the need for households to reduce their debt burdens; contractionary fiscal policy at all levels of government after the initial effects of the fiscal stimulus package had passed; and elevated uncertainty about the economic outlook that made firms hesitant to invest and hire, and households reluctant to buy houses, cars, and other discretionary goods.

Fortunately, the overall force of these headwinds appears to have diminished considerably over the past year or so, allowing employment to accelerate appreciably even as the level of the federal funds rate and the volume of our asset holdings remained nearly unchanged.[6] Stated differently, the economy's underlying strength has been

---

[6] Although the FOMC suspended its asset purchase program last October, the stimulus provided by this type of unconventional monetary policy action depends primarily on the stock of longer-term assets held by the Federal Reserve, not the flow of securities bought. Because the FOMC has held the size of the Federal Reserve's balance sheet constant since October while continuing to keep the federal funds rate near zero, the overall stance of monetary policy is thus little changed over this period. However, the downward pressure on long-term interest rates from the Federal Reserve's asset holdings should decline over time, particularly after the FOMC suspends its current reinvestment policy, because the average duration of the assets held in the portfolio will be steadily falling and because the relative size of the portfolio to the stock of publicly held debt will be shrinking.

gradually improving, and the equilibrium real federal funds rate has been gradually

rising. Although the recent appreciation of the dollar is likely to weigh on U.S. exports

over time, I nonetheless anticipate further diminution of the headwinds just noted over

the next couple of years, and as the equilibrium real funds rate continues to rise, it will

accordingly be appropriate to raise the actual level of the real federal funds rate in

tandem, all else being equal.[7] At present, the equilibrium real federal funds rate, which

by some estimates is currently close to zero, appears to be well below the longer-run

normal levels assessed by the FOMC. The median SEP estimate of this longer-run

normal rate--that is, the long-run projection of the nominal funds rate less 2 percent

inflation--stood at 1-3/4 percent in the FOMC's recent projections.[8] Provided that

inflation shows clear signs over time of moving up toward 2 percent in the context of

continuing progress toward maximum employment, I therefore expect that a further

tightening in monetary policy after the first increase in the federal funds rate will be

warranted. Should incoming data, however, fail to support this forecast, then the actual

path of policy will need to be adjusted appropriately.

---

[7] If resource utilization was at a normal level and inflation was equal to 2 percent, policymakers would presumably opt to set the real federal funds rate equal to the equilibrium real rate in order to maintain those conditions. Accordingly, if the equilibrium rate is rising over time, the "neutral" setting of monetary policy should be rising in tandem.

[8] For example, the estimate of the equilibrium real rate from the Laubach-Williams model for 2014:Q4 is negative 0.16. For information on the model, see Thomas Laubach and John C. Williams (2003), "Measuring the Natural Rate of Interest," *Review of Economics and Statistics,* vol. 85 (November), pp. 1063-70; updated estimates of the baseline model are available on the Federal Reserve Bank of San Francisco website at www.frbsf.org/economic-research/economists/john-williams/Laubach_Williams_updated_estimates.xlsx. Another recent study, however, concludes that the equilibrium real rate is probably in the range of 1 to 2 percent while also emphasizing that estimates in this area are quite imprecise; see James D. Hamilton, Ethan S. Harris, Jan Hatzius, and Kenneth D. West (2015), "The Equilibrium Real Funds Rate: Past, Present, and Future," working paper (San Diego: University of California at San Diego, March), http://econweb.ucsd.edu/~jhamilto/USMPF_2015.pdf. Note that the concept of the equilibrium real rate used in the latter study is explicitly long-run in nature and so excludes the effects of forces that have persistently restrained the pace of the current expansion but are expected to eventually fade away, such as household balance sheet repair; for this reason, the paper's estimate is higher than the medium-run concept of the equilibrium real rate discussed in the speech.

Are There Special Risks and Other Considerations That Policymakers Should Take into Account in the Current Environment?

As I noted, my FOMC colleagues and I generally anticipate that a rather gradual rise in the federal funds rate will be appropriate over the next few years, conditional on our baseline forecasts for real activity, inflation, and other aspects of the economy's performance. So far in my remarks, I have emphasized one key rationale for such a judgment--namely, that the equilibrium real federal funds rate is at present well below its historical average and is anticipated to rise only gradually over time as the various headwinds that have restrained the economic recovery continue to abate. If incoming data support such a forecast, the federal funds rate should be normalized, but at a gradual pace.

Several additional factors reinforce this conclusion, and that brings me to my third question: Are there special risks and other considerations that policymakers should take into account in the current environment? Keeping in mind that the actual course of monetary policy in the future will primarily depend on events as they unfold, I see three additional considerations that are relevant.[9]

The first, which is closely related to my expectation that the headwinds holding back growth are likely to continue to abate gradually, pertains to the risk that the equilibrium real federal funds rate may not, in fact, recover as much or as quickly as I

---

[9] In principle, the three considerations--uncertainty about the value of the equilibrium real federal funds rate, the asymmetric risks associated with the zero lower bound on nominal interest rates, and the potential benefits of allowing the unemployment rate to temporarily undershoot its sustainable longer-run rate-- should influence both the timing of the onset of policy normalization and the subsequent pace at which that normalization proceeds. And in fact, I view all three considerations as helping to explain why the FOMC has held the federal funds rate near zero for so long. I also view such considerations as consistent with a likely increase in the target federal funds rate later this year, because such an increase would be part of a broader strategy for only gradually reducing accommodation over time (subject, of course, to adjustments in response to incoming information on real activity, inflation, and other factors).

anticipate. Substantial uncertainty surrounds all estimates of the equilibrium real interest rate, and, as I will discuss momentarily, market participants appear to be fairly pessimistic about the odds that it will rise significantly over time. Moreover, some recent studies have raised the prospect that the economies of the United States and other countries will grow more slowly in the future as a result of both demographic factors and a slower pace of productivity gains from technological advances. At an extreme, such developments could even amount to a type of "secular stagnation," in which monetary policy would need to keep real interest rates persistently quite low relative to historical norms to promote full employment and price stability, absent a highly expansive fiscal policy.[10]

Such a risk has important implications for monetary policy in the near term, when the ability of the economy to adjust to significant rate increases will be especially uncertain. The experience of Japan over the past 20 years, and Sweden more recently, demonstrates that a tightening of policy when the equilibrium real rate remains low can result in appreciable economic costs, delaying the attainment of a central bank's price stability objective. International experience therefore counsels caution in removing accommodation until the Committee is more confident that aggregate demand will

---

[10] The concept of "secular stagnation" was first coined back in the late 1930s; see Alvin H. Hansen (1938), "The Consequences of Reducing Expenditures," *Proceedings of the Academy of Political Science*, vol. 17 (January), pp. 60-72; and Alvin H. Hansen (1939), "Economic Progress and Declining Population Growth," *American Economic Review*, vol. 29 (March), pp. 1-15. This possibility, and its applicability to the United States and other developed economies in coming years, has received considerable attention of late; see Robert J. Gordon (2014), "The Demise of U.S. Economic Growth: Restatement, Rebuttal, and Reflections," NBER Working Paper Series 19895 (Cambridge, Mass.: National Bureau of Economic Research, February); Robert E. Hall (2014), "Quantifying the Lasting Harm to the U.S. Economy from the Financial Crisis," in Jonathan Parker and Michael Woodford, eds., *NBER Macroeconomics Annual,* vol. 29 (Chicago: University of Chicago Press); and Lawrence H. Summers (2014), "U.S. Economic Prospects: Secular Stagnation, Hysteresis, and the Zero Lower Bound," *Business Economics*, vol. 49 (April), pp. 65-73. For a more skeptical assessment of the secular stagnation hypothesis, see Hamilton and others, "The Equilibrium Real Funds Rate," in note 8.

continue to expand in line with its expectations--a view that is also supported by the research literature.[11]

A second reason for the Committee to proceed cautiously in removing policy accommodation relates to asymmetries in the effectiveness of monetary policy in the vicinity of the zero lower bound. In the event that growth in employment and overall activity proves unexpectedly robust and inflation moves significantly above our 2 percent objective, the FOMC can and will raise interest rates as needed to rein in inflation. But if growth was to falter and inflation was to fall yet further, the effective lower bound on nominal interest rates could limit the Committee's ability to provide the needed degree of accommodation. With an already large balance sheet, for example, the FOMC might be concerned about potential costs and risks associated with further asset purchases.

Research suggests that, the higher the probability of monetary policy becoming constrained by the zero lower bound in the near future because of adverse shocks, and the more severe the attendant consequences for real activity and inflation, the more current policy should lean in accommodative direction.[12] In effect, such a strategy represents insurance against the zero lower bound by aiming for somewhat stronger real activity and

---

[11] A number of studies have shown, using model simulations, that policymakers can improve macroeconomic performance by adjusting the stance of monetary policy more cautiously in response to changes in economic conditions when the economy's equilibrium real interest rate is uncertain. For a survey of the literature on this issue, see John B. Taylor and John C. Williams (2010), "Simple and Robust Rules for Monetary Policy," in Benjamin M. Friedman and Michael Woodford, eds., *Handbook of Monetary Economics,* vol. 3B (San Diego: Elsevier), pp. 829-59.

[12] For example, see Klaus Adam and Roberto M. Billi (2007), "Discretionary Monetary Policy and the Zero Lower Bound on Nominal Interest Rates," *Journal of Monetary Economics*, vol. 54 (3), 728-52; Taisuke Nakata (2013), "Optimal Fiscal and Monetary Policy with Occasionally Binding Zero Bound Constraints," Finance and Economics Discussion Series 2013-40 (Washington: Board of Governors of the Federal Reserve System, April), www.federalreserve.gov/pubs/feds/2013/201340/201340pap.pdf; Taisuke Nakata (2013), "Uncertainty at the Zero Lower Bound," Finance and Economics Discussion Series 2013-09 (Washington: Board of Governors of the Federal Reserve System, December 2012), www.federalreserve.gov/pubs/feds/2013/201309/201309pap.pdf; and Charles Evans, Jonas Fisher, Francois Gourio, and Spencer Krane (forthcoming), "Risk Management for Monetary Policy Near the Zero Lower Bound," Brookings Papers on Economic Activity (Washington: Brookings Institution).

a faster rise in inflation under the modal outlook. Given the modal outlook envisioned in FOMC participants' recent forecasts, with headwinds continuing to diminish, the equilibrium real rate rising, and inflation moving back up to 2 percent over the next few years, the risk that the funds rate would need to return to near zero should be declining appreciably. Consistent with this assessment, almost all FOMC participants now view the risks to the outlook for real activity as largely balanced, although some also see inflation risks as weighted to the downside.

That said, it is sobering to note that many market participants appear to assess the risks to the outlook quite differently. For example, respondents to the Survey of Primary Dealers in late January thought there was a 20 percent probability that, after liftoff, the funds rate would fall back to zero sometime at or before late 2017.[13] In addition, both the remarkably low level of long-term government bond yields in advanced economies and the low prevailing level of inflation compensation suggest that financial market participants may hold more pessimistic views than FOMC participants concerning the risks to the global outlook. Since long-term yields reflect the market's probability-weighted average of all possible short-term interest rate paths, along with compensating term and risk premiums, the generally low level of yields in advanced economies suggests that investors place considerable odds on adverse scenarios that would necessitate a lower and flatter trajectory of the federal funds than envisioned in participants' modal SEP projections.[14]

---

[13] See Federal Reserve Bank of New York, Markets Group (2015), *Responses to Survey of Primary Dealers* (New York: FRBNY, January), www.newyorkfed.org/markets/survey/2015/January-result.pdf.

[14] Of course, low long-term yields in the United States may not reflect investor pessimism about U.S. economic prospects but instead an expectation that weak economic performance abroad may result in persistent upward pressure on the dollar, thereby putting downward pressure on U.S. net exports, employment, inflation, and thus short-term interest rates. On a closely related issue concerning evidence that investors' perceptions of the likelihood of high inflation versus low inflation have shifted noticeably in

A final argument for gradually adjusting policy relates to the desirability of achieving a prompt return of inflation to the FOMC's 2 percent goal, an objective that would be advanced by allowing the unemployment rate to decline for a time somewhat below estimates of its longer-run sustainable level. To a limited degree, such an outcome is envisioned in many participants' most recent SEP projections. A tight labor market may also work to reverse some of the adverse supply-side developments resulting from the financial crisis. The deep recession and slow recovery likely have held back investment in physical and human capital, restrained the rate of new business formation, prompted discouraged workers to leave the labor force, and eroded the skills of the long-term unemployed.[15] Some of these effects might be reversed in a tight labor market, yielding long-term benefits associated with a more productive economy. That said, the quantitative importance of these supply-side mechanisms are difficult to establish, and the relevant research on this point is quite limited.

Of course, taking a gradualist approach is not without risks. Proceeding too slowly to tighten policy could have adverse consequences for the attainment of the Committee's inflation objective over time, especially if it were to undermine the FOMC's inflation credibility. Inflation could, for example, exhibit nonlinear dynamics in which high levels of unemployment place relatively little downward pressure on inflation, but tight labor markets generate marked upward pressure. If so, a decline in unemployment

recent months, see Justin Wolfers (2015), "A Prediction Market for Inflation, or Deflation," The Upshot, *New York Times,* March 6. This piece relies heavily on work by Yuriy Kitsul and Jonathan H. Wright (2013), "The Economics of Options-Implied Inflation Probability Density Functions," *Journal of Financial Economics*, vol. 110 (December), 696-711.

[15] For a discussion of these effects, see Dave Reifschneider, William Wascher, and David Wilcox (2015), "Aggregate Supply in the United States: Recent Developments and Implications for the Conduct of Monetary Policy," *IMF Economic Review* advance online publication, March 17, doi: 10.1057/imfer.2015.1.

below its natural rate could cause inflation to quickly rise to an undesirably high level. Rapid increases in short-term interest rates to arrest such an unwelcome development could, in turn, have adverse effects on financial markets and the broader economy.

Proceeding too cautiously could also have undesirable effects on financial stability. An environment of prolonged low short-term rates could prompt an excessive buildup in leverage or cause underwriting standards to erode as investors take on risks they cannot measure or manage appropriately in a reach for yield.[16] At this point the evidence indicates that such vulnerabilities do not pose a significant threat, but the Committee is carefully monitoring developments in this area.[17] Moreover, in my view, macroprudential regulatory and supervisory tools should serve as our first line of defense in addressing these risks.[18]

Conclusion

To conclude, let me emphasize that in determining when to initially increase its target range for the federal funds rate and how to adjust it thereafter, the Committee's decisions will be data dependent, reflecting evolving judgments concerning the implications of incoming information for the economic outlook. We cannot be certain about the underlying strength of the expansion, the maximum level of employment consistent with price stability, or the longer-run level of interest rates consistent with

---

[16] Jeremy C. Stein (2013), "Overheating in Credit Markets: Origins, Measurement, and Policy Responses," speech delivered at "Restoring Household Financial Stability after the Great Recession: Why Household Balance Sheets Matter," a research symposium sponsored by the Federal Reserve Bank of St. Louis, St. Louis, February 7, www.federalreserve.gov/newsevents/speech/stein20130207a.htm.

[17] See Janet L. Yellen (2014), "Semiannual Monetary Policy Report to the Congress," testimony before the Committee on Banking, Housing, and Urban Affairs, U.S. Senate, July 15, www.federalreserve.gov/newsevents/testimony/yellen20140715a.htm.

[18] See Janet L. Yellen, (2014) "Monetary Policy and Financial Stability," speech delivered at the 2014 Michel Camdessus Central Banking Lecture, International Monetary Fund, Washington, July 2, www.federalreserve.gov/newsevents/speech/yellen20140702a.htm.

maximum employment. Policy must adjust as our understanding of these factors

changes. However, if conditions do evolve in the manner that most of my FOMC

colleagues and I anticipate, I would expect the level of the federal funds rate to be

normalized only gradually, reflecting the gradual diminution of headwinds from the

financial crisis and the balance of risks I have enumerated of moving either too slowly or

too quickly. Nothing about the course of the Committee's actions is predetermined

except the Committee's commitment to promote our dual mandate of maximum

employment and price stability.